September Love

ALSO BY LANG LEAV

FICTION
Sad Girls
Poemsia

POETRY
Love & Misadventure
Lullabies
Memories
The Universe of Us
Sea of Strangers
Love Looks Pretty on You

September Love

LANG LEAV

Andrews McMeel
PUBLISHING®

Andrews McMeel Publishing
a division of Andrews McMeel Universal
1130 Walnut Street, Kansas City, Missouri 64106

www.andrewsmcmeel.com

20 21 22 23 24 RR2 10 9 8 7 6 5 4 3 2 1

ISBN: 978-1-5248-5959-6

Library of Congress Control Number: 2020942677

Editor: Patty Rice
Art Director/Designer: Diane Marsh
Production Editor: Dave Shaw
Production Manager: Cliff Koehler

ATTENTION: SCHOOLS AND BUSINESSES
Andrews McMeel books are available at quantity
discounts with bulk purchase for educational, business, or
sales promotional use. For information, please e-mail the
Andrews McMeel Publishing Special Sales Department:
specialsales@amuniversal.com.

For Michael,
my September Love.

Foreword by Lili Reinhart

I believe we read poetry to connect to the world around us. I would argue that the most important and valuable aspect of life is human connection. My love of poetry blossomed when I was sixteen as I started reading poems as a form of therapy. I remember discovering Lang's work on Tumblr, where I constantly scoured the site in search of love poems to send to my long-distance boyfriend at the time. Her delicate, soft font first caught my eye, but it was the beauty and depth that Lang created with such few words that had the greatest influence on me.

Sharing your poetry with the world is comparable to opening up your journal, full of your deepest vulnerabilities and desires, and allowing the world to read. As a writer myself, I have a deep appreciation for my fellow poets who share the words that stem from their open hearts. It is a raw and humbling experience, and Lang was kind enough to reach out to me with support and encouragement when I announced the publication of my first collection.

Lang's words seem as if they are individually plucked with precision and purpose, thoughtfully portraying a picture that lives inside her mind. She looks back on her own emotions and experiences with such clarity, and you can see her deep appreciation for the ability to feel so profoundly. Writing poetry has a way of revealing your innermost fears and desires, and it is one of our greatest resources in learning about ourselves: "To hold tight each feeling I am blessed to have felt, I write not to be known but to know myself."

I read Lang's collection during a period of global unrest and uncertainty, a time when the future was unclear and "normal" didn't exist anymore. It was also a time when I was coming out on the other side of a long, harrowing grieving process. I felt an overwhelming rush of empathy in reading her poems. It was like looking straight into her heart, and seeing my own heart silhouetted underneath. I recognized myself in her experiences. I saw my pain in her words. And that's the whole point of poetry, isn't it? To see yourself in someone else. To feel less alone.

Our world needs poetry more than ever right now, as we struggle to find connection across distances and differences. In bringing universal emotions to life, Lang reminds us that we all have more in common than we might otherwise imagine. And perhaps the most powerful thing we share—as she writes so beautifully in the poem that gives this collection its title—is a sense of a yearning, that singular emotion that looks longingly to the past and dreamily toward the future: "how long do we go on dragging our bodies day after day through this yawning, yearning world, searching for a glimpse of what could have been?"

September Love
(Originally published in Sea of Strangers*)*

How many years must we put between us to prove we are no longer in love? How many summers and Septembers, distractions and chance meetings, remnants of our sad, hopeful love in another's look, an all too familiar gesture—how long do we go on dragging our bodies day after day through this yawning, yearning world, searching for a glimpse of what could have been?

Tell me there has been someone else like me, for you. That your experience of love has not been defined by the way I spoke your name into the hollow of your neck. Ask me if I have found the same kind of reverence anywhere else but in your slow, patient hands, your sea-salt lips spilling laughter mid-sentence, my heart rising in a crescendo like a wave ready to crash.

As you whispered to me, *love is the only thing that time cannot touch.*

After all this time, my love for you burns constant and true, my guiding light, my morning star. Time is testament to the relentless, unyielding power of this old, ancient love. A love I will carry with me, from eons to oceans to inches, back to you.

I'm Sorry

To the poem I put
into a book
before it was ready
I'm sorry I didn't wait
a few lines longer

To the flowers
I picked before
they were ready
When sunlight
still shone
like a prayer
on their petals
I'm sorry

To the man I will
love and love
until the word love
no longer means
anything to anyone
I'm sorry I wasn't ready

Dear February

You were always the month of goodbyes
standing sentry to autumn and her changing hues
Tall trees and dappled light on the city pavement
shifting under my feet, skirting the cracks
I think of my mother and what she lost one February
and there are things you know about me
that I don't want her to know
Is my secret safe with you, dear February?
Like you I am caught between the city lights and the sea
torn between my love and my home
Like you I am the sun that keeps setting too soon
missing the summer even while I'm here

Self-Preservation

I used to think love had no limits—but I draw the line at myself.

Ingredients of a Poem

Someone you miss
The whir of a blade
A half-checked list

A cake made to savor
Someone's misfortune
That swings in your favor

The clock on the hour
The run of the mill
Love that has soured

The close of a fist
The start of a book
Whatever you wish

Motherhood

Your name is the second one
your mother gave you

Love was the first

Who You Are

He has you, words tangled, wings clipped, folded at your breast. Trapped within yourself thinking, *how did I get here?* With all your promise and intellect, *how did I get here?* Whittled down like this, reduced to something you swore you'd never be. Now, how do you tear yourself away from him without ripping your life to shreds? You no longer recognize yourself, but sweet girl, that means you still know who you are. And while there is still a glimmer of hope behind those sad, tired eyes, know he hasn't worn you down. And while there is an ounce of fight left in you, know he hasn't won just yet. And while there is a chance in hell you get out of this, you come out swinging.

More a Poet

I fell asleep to the rain last night
And the sun came to me in a dream
Beaming down on me, sweeter than anything
More real to me than skin

A voice I knew as yours said to me
One day I woke up and with every breath
I thought of you

And I wanted to tell you
I thought of you too. You said
Nothing went wrong with us; we just let go
But you and I—we are eternal—okay?

By the time my eyes fluttered open
It was already daylight. And I found myself
Drenched in poetry. That morning I was
more a poet than I had ever been

Outside my window, it had been raining forever
And then the sun came quietly back

Always Will

Here we are, fantasizing about normality. Our world has turned on its axis and we have all been thrown into the air, not knowing where we'll land. Wondering if there will still be a place for us among the ruins. Yes, we took it all for granted—but isn't that such a blessed thing? When you're not even thinking about what you have, because you never imagine you someday won't.

Why I Write

I write without knowing
whom my words will find
without thinking further
than the next line

When my heart grows
too heavy to hold—I write
from the depth of my sorrow
to dizzying heights

I write without dreams
of awards or applause
but for the joy of rendering
my soul into words

To hold tight each feeling
I am blessed to have felt
I write not to be known
but to know myself

Limbo

When you wait for a man to make up his mind about you, your life cannot move forward. You can't put your whole heart in anything else if you're betting on something that may not come through. You can build the life of your dreams without him. You can start today. But first, you need to take your heart off the table. You have a few precious years to do what you need to do. Don't waste them on him.

Twice in My Life

Twice in my life
I was mistaken
for someone else
Twice in my life
an imposter came
and took my place

The first time
it was my second love
It was someone I loved

The second time
it was my first love
There was nothing I loved
before I loved poetry

And what I loved
before I loved
will wage a war for me
As I walk among
the false idols
and fallen angels
the truth will give itself
to the light

The first time, my love
you will never know
how much I loved
The second time
all the world will know

The Age of Love

People ask me how old I am, and I smile. It is impolite to ask a woman her age. But I don't mind at all. I tell them I am merely growing into my skin, that I have always been an old soul, and they ask me,

doesn't your soul remain the age you were when you first fell in love?

Well, I answer, *love is older than time,* and then I tell them about you—and how I have loved you for a very, very long time.

Seasons

If you were to choose a season, which would it be?
The golden dunes of summer, wild and free
The quiet breath of winter—trees bare and stark
Or spring's flowers and her honeybees?

Would you swim in the ocean or walk in the park?
Or catch the sunset before it grows dark?
What page of the calendar would you mark?
I'd choose fall—the season you came back to me

Fleeting

All love is fleeting—even when it lasts a lifetime

Only So Much

There is only so much you can say about a man who hurts you so covertly, so gradually. The tiny paper cuts that come one after another, so measured and subdued. It barely hurts, until it does. Yet your pain is visible to no one, sometimes, not even to yourself. There is no blood to mop up, no broken glass to sweep. Not a trace of anything untoward until it gets too much, and suddenly you are a wild animal thrashing, baring your teeth, and when they ask you why, you have nothing to show, no answer to give.

Grief

Grief is like a flower
the way it blooms
and blooms. It is
a heart-shaped wound

that never closes
A mouth, always wanting
More love is found in grief
than in love itself

Like a diamond
that can only be cut
with another diamond
grief is the only thing
that cuts through love

Between Us

There is always something between us, my love: a closed door, an endless corridor, a locked screen. There you are under the lamppost at dusk. Is it summer or are we still in spring? I can see you across the road, arms above your head waving hello. In my chest, something crashes hard as a head-on collision. And suddenly you grow further away like gravity turned on its side, you are up, and I am down. Here comes the feeling of falling I'd forgotten, tried to bury beneath the years. Do you see me anymore, my dear, do you trust yourself now? Does it make you smile to know you were right about me all along, somewhere deep down, does it kill you?

A Life Unlived

We reminisce so much about the past that it becomes like a second shadow. We dream so much about the future that we are hardly present.

We talk so much about our lives, we forget to live it.

Twenty Nineteen

This year broke like a ray of sun on rain; hope that pierced my heart like an ache. Brought the promise of a new beginning; a chance to set things right. But it came with the same old sadness, the same betrayals, the inescapable turmoil of my life. The peaks and valleys of my days, like the line of a pulse shooting up so high, I thought nothing would ever touch me again, and then so low that nothing could.

This year found new ways to break my heart but I didn't let it break me. Gave as much as it took and still left me wanting. Left me with a proud, unwavering sense of myself, and a fierce, unbreakable resolve to conquer the next.

Let It

I have a rule about not thinking where I am or what comes next. I guess when you let go of the need to know, everything tends to fall into place. It is okay to dream, to allow your higher self to take care of the rest.

So, if something is calling you, answer. If it bursts out of your chest like a trapped bird set free, follow it. There is a mysterious pull that longs to take you exactly where you need to go. Let it.

All I See

Did you say I am the girl who reads too much into everything—that I can't look at a word without seeing a poem—or turn a flower into a field? I never see things as they are, only what they could be. So, can you blame me when I look at you and all I see is love.

Locked Boxes

My mind is filled with keys
and locked boxes

With every turn I hear
the click of a pen

In every box
there is a poem

Crystal Ball

When I look back on my life, it is so easy to see how every decision could have led me elsewhere. And if only I'd had the gift of hindsight, I could have changed it for the better. But how could I have known that crystal balls are just a skewed reflection of our present? So now I am standing here, wondering what direction I should go in. Looking, looking for what I'm not seeing.

For a Man

My absolute love and adoration for a man can live in peace
with my feminism.

Nine Books

The first book was a song that came from nowhere. The second and third bloomed like a garden I kept in secret. By the fourth, something dark was brewing. I lost my way at five, six, and seven. By eight I wanted blood. Here at nine I am back to the sweet insistent singing from where it started. Never has my voice echoed so freely. Drawn from the well of my soul. And I will always sing like this from now on. Even if I'm the only one who hears it.

In Love and Free

In every relationship, there is an underlying question we must keep asking ourselves:

How can we at once be in love and free?

Give You

I give you up, fingernails dug in dirt
spitting up blood, I give you up
like the sea gives up her dead
like a string of pearls falling to pieces
crashing onto the cold hard floor
on my hands and knees, scraping up the mess
a rush of Hail Marys raining from my mouth
and I would imagine this isn't love
but some other beast altogether
and if they asked me if I could have died
happy never knowing a world where
you don't want me, I would say yes
They tell me love is something
I have to claw my way out of
Breaking through bone, tearing through skin
Stripping myself of everything
in this final show of my devotion to you
my everything—the only thing left I can give you
I can give you—give you up

April Fool

We came together in July, clung to one another like leaves to a tree, everything golden before the fall. My love was a bird feathering her nest, spring in my heart, perched on a branch, singing. Your love was a question that never found an answer—still hasn't. I held on for as long as I could until I was stripped bare of everything you thought you wanted, and you couldn't look at me the way you used to. Do you think what sparked between us was love—or just another beautiful trick of the light? I was your April fool—just three months shy of a year with you. Arms open and waiting, waiting for the seaside promise of summer, never once doubting it would come.

A Poem Comes

This was a poem that came to me
the way anything good comes
Like a comet that swings back around
or a recipe you reconstruct
from a childhood memory
The lens with which you peer through
all blurred and sentimental

It came to me through the
lifelong wonder I've held
of the way words will unravel
if you let them, as though they
are creating these sentient worlds
entirely on their own

The Gift

It was a crisp, bright day as I walked to my apartment, wanting nothing more than I had. By the threshold, a man twelve paces in front suddenly stopped—bent down to pick something up. With his back to me, he inspected it carefully, then slipped it into his pocket. I wondered what it was that lay twelve steps down the pavement, some small luminous gift from the sky. I thought about this strange and mysterious offering, what it could be, and how it had almost been mine.

If You Didn't

If you didn't know me
you would see me as they do
believe the lies they tell
about me were true

If you didn't know me
you wouldn't want to know me—
I would never be
the one for you

And you wouldn't be sorry
for missing what you never knew
If you didn't know me—
only, my love, you do

Endless Thirst

You are at once a sea full of saltwater, and the endless thirst scratching the back of my throat.

Diorama

Tell me about your life, they say
Do you really want to know about me?
Not the meticulous shopfront of my life
the grinning dolls in the window
forever youthful propped up with pills
The surgeon's scalpel making me more
what I'm supposed to be, less who I am
Where I'm from there is a name
for women like me
Women who slip into the lives of others
transient, even if they never leave
Who give all they have to a man
and thank him for the privilege

Do you really want to hear about the raised eyebrows
the humiliation of being seen as less than I am
the desperation of proving myself at every party
where someone needs to say in colorful tones
oh, she is someone because if I wasn't
then I'd just be another eye roll
the absent shake of the head
women grasping the hands of their husbands
a little tighter when I'm in close proximity

I tell them about my life by the sea
the idyllic writer's life, the bohemian glitz
of never having to sing for my supper
lying around in bed all day in my pajamas
petting cats, eating out of cereal boxes
and the thing I want to say is the very thing I can't

Because this is not my life
and I know it looks beautiful to you
through the rose-tinted lens of poetry
it looks beautiful to you when every light is on
and the shades are up.

It looks beautiful to you with my head thrown back
easy laughter spilling from my mouth
my arms wrapped around a man
solely devoted to my happiness
his fingers through my hair, watching me
and you think, look at her
so much love, so much life

But only from the outside
Only when someone's looking in

Fallen Idols

I wish I could go back to a time when I only believed good things about you

To past generations,

You grew up in a time of tall trees and flowers. Stumbled through the dark, blameless and carefree. When you were at fault, you answered only to yourself. The pain you've caused others—now inconsequential—because no one was watching. You belong to a world of forgotten transgressions.

Our generation blooms in the era of eyes and judgment. Where our mistakes are timestamped; our broken hearts livestreamed. But does this give you a right to throw stones at us? Self-growth is a long and winding road, and the ground we are treading is unlike any other. Please be patient with us. Be kind. Understand that we must lose our way, over and over, before we can find the best version of ourselves.

Self-Blame

I can't deny this is all my fault. I have no one else to blame for my life falling to pieces. But let me ask you this: is pain any less valid when it is self-inflicted?

Doesn't it hurt just as much?

Want

What do you long for
in your heart of hearts
in this eruption of light
between eons of dark

What do you wish for
at the cut of the cake
A knife in your hand
for a love you still ache

You'll get what you want
if you're willing to wait
If not when you want it
then when it's too late

Either Or

There is so much anxiety in the beginning. So much hope and faith. But it's all unnecessary. Once you give your heart away, it's out of your hands. And there's nothing you can do to change the fact that love is, or it isn't. It will either work or it won't.

The Golden Rule

Something I wish I had known from the beginning. If you are criticized for your writing, it means you are creating work of note. When you find yourself in a place where strangers are talking about you, keep creating the work that got you noticed. Do not alter your writing to appease your critics. It is natural to crave validation, especially from those who will never give it. To be a successful writer, you must ignore this instinct. This is the most critical lesson I have learned. You can't please everyone, so don't even try. This rule applies in life, in love, and especially in writing.

Only Yours

In this poem
there is only one voice
My voice and none other

In every other poem
there is only one other
One voice other than mine
There is only your voice and mine

Hidden Love

Just like you would hide a tree in a forest, I hide my love in a poem.

Being an Artist

I recall those lonely nights
pushing pixels on my screen
craving pencil and paper
the smear of paint
beneath my fingertips
the sound of paper sighing
as I drew a line

I dreamt of being an artist
just enough to eat and live
Just enough for the little things
A cup of coffee with a friend
on a park bench one sunny day
A vase full of flowers
I put on my shelf to admire
or a book I can devour slowly
over two weekends

It was a lifetime ago
when I thought of all the things
I could do if only I didn't
have to chase the things I need
And now here I am with more time
than I had ever dreamt
I pick up my pencil
and nothing comes

Of Years

One day, love came to me. And love has remained with me since. How long was it, before I noticed the ebbing of years? Like a thief in the night, taking so little at a time—it seemed like hardly anything at all.

To the Guy Who Claims My Poetry Was the Cause
of His Break-up,

It is astonishing to think that my words have the power to make someone fall out of love with you. That I have somehow been conspiring against you, even though up until this moment, I was blissfully unaware of your existence. Maybe you should ask yourself why she has found her self-worth in the words of others and not yours. Could it be, perhaps, that I'm not some grand puppet master like you believe, that my words are not a cold hard slap, but merely, a soft tap on the shoulder and the truth is—you're just a shitty boyfriend?

The World Is Mine

Something imperceptible has shifted
like a stone lodged between two worlds
Shook loose with barely a sigh
I lost my way for awhile
but I am back where I belong
Every sound and syllable trembles with meaning
Words rearranging themselves for me
In an ever-changing dance
This is the end of an endless drought
The rain streams down my cheeks
I weep with joy
Throw my hands in the air
Everything is righting itself
and the world is mine again

Taking Time

I need a day of nothing, a reprieve from the spinning merry-go-round of my life. Shrug it off like an old winter coat and hang it by the door. I need a day where I am not asked, wanted, or noticed. To know there is a wall of silence between me and everything else.

Self-Control

I am rewriting this
to sound less
like a complaint
Lowering my voice
so I won't be dismissed

I've long since learned
what I say is second
to how I say it
Learned to level
my voice, when I
am screaming
on the inside

This is what it is
to be a woman
To learn how to
swallow your pain
To know how
to bide your time

Tongue-Tied

I am a sentence strung together out of sequence, written for your tongue to untangle.

No Poet

There is no poet before me who is exactly as I am. No one will ever write the words I've written, think the thoughts I've thought. My poetry is a candle burning gently, an everlasting flame coaxing something tender, turning all toward love. So much of our world is drenched in anger. But love is our natural state of being. We may lose our way for awhile, but from love we have come and to love we will return.

In a World Like That

I don't want to be in a relationship where I feel the constant need to explain myself. I don't want to live in a world like that either.

War

Are you a man of peace? I ask you.

You will see one day there is no such thing. In the end, your noble ideals will fall victim to circumstance. Something in your life will reveal with all certainty the ugly truth of men.

And how it is only a question of time until, like every other man before you,

(you will see)

you will come face-to-face with that thing for which you will go to war.

The Path of a Writer

The path of a writer starts with an electric pulse, like a heartbeat. Barely perceptible and fragile as a newborn. Someone once told me writing is like panning for gold. But I think it is like stumbling on the ruins of a lost city, talking to its ghosts. Wandering its deserted streets with long-forgotten names.

One day you will find your city and you will build it with one painstaking word after another. Only then will you know the path of a writer. Know what it is truly like to inhabit a world you have created, and how this world that began as a heartbeat, becomes a living, breathing thing.

Only Once

Love comes easy when you're young
and you can be forgiven for thinking
love is like rain, and rain is relentless

But at the end of your life—if ever
you find yourself thinking about love
then you never did see its return

Because you can't really comprehend
not at first—that anything in this world
that comes that easy, only comes once

Before Love

The night my world crashed into his, I belonged to no one. By the time I collapsed into bed, the sun was already on her way. My body throbbed to the phantom music ringing in my ears. My feet ached from dancing the whole night long. And I couldn't stop smiling.

That was the moment before everything.

When I thought I was in love—when I had yet to feel the full force of it.

Before You Leave

Before you leave in the morning
remember what you've left
The girl you swore your heart to
the dream you held as you slept

Before the evening carries you
to the dawn of another day
think of how you'd miss her
as you go on your way

Before the sun goes down again
and you resign yourself to fate
know that it is in your hands
before it gets too late

Not You

I don't want the best thing to come too early in my life

I hope with all my heart it wasn't you

Too Close

I live my life between being loved
or being known
wishing the two were one

To be loved is a wave rushing past
the shoreline; filling every void
To be known is an ache
that never goes away

Now that you love me, are you afraid
to know me? Will distance tell you
what your heart refuses to see?

You're too close to me, my love
You're missing everything

A Woman

The day you become a woman, they hand you a grenade. And you must choose between hurling or holding. Between want and expectation. Excise your desire, while you are hungry for everything. Give up your life for a version of you that isn't you at all.

Do not think twice about the imposition when they tell you, *there is nothing worse than a fallen woman. Nothing worse than a woman who doesn't know her place.* You will learn otherwise when you trade your truth for an ideal that no amount of good you do will ever be enough anyway.

So, make up your own rules. Don't be afraid to hurl, to fall, to get dirt on your face. Sweetheart, let this be your one glorious mess because in the end the only person you should answer to is yourself.

After all, you are a woman,

And long before they punish you for what you've done, they will punish you for what you are.

Breaking

I feel a crack inside—
the sound of something breaking
I know this feeling well

I want to self-destruct
Burn my whole life to the ground
I've been here before
I know how it goes

This is the only way
I know how to be
There are no words left
and nothing is growing

Legacy

You must believe it is your destiny to create beauty in this world. To shape your life with love and purpose, touch it ever so briefly with your weary hands and leave it a little more cherished than it was.

Losing

You are losing control
You are losing yourself
That man is your downfall
your ticket to hell

But his hands are like black magic
This isn't love but God
it's almost as good

Like some hell-bent force
that has kept you away
from everything you want
Swinging like a lead ball
all the way back
and it's too much

The secret is
no one gets what they want
without losing who they are

The One After

You've lived your whole life with me, haven't you, my love?
Yet I don't think you've truly seen me once. I am a projection
of the girl who hurt you, a conduit of the pain she caused.
After all this time, I am still being punished simply for being
the one who came after.

Like It Was

You've waited so long
for someone you can laugh with
even when you're sad

Someone you can be at
peace with, even with
a stomach full of butterflies

And as you are searching
the great sea of darkness
for a flicker of light
there is someone who is
searching for you

One day you will find refuge
in another, and they will learn
to know your heart
like it was their own

My Poetry

They accuse me of never putting myself on a page, that I distance myself from my poetry like an old lover I have lived to regret. They say I'm dishonest, inauthentic, that I don't know heartbreak the way I write it. But there are other ways to tell my secrets, and I have many. Like apple seeds buried deep in my bones. Cinnamon and cyanide. Blood pacts and promises. There are so many versions of me splashed onto a page, like a carnival of mirrors. I wanted you to know my poetry, but I never meant for you to know me.

God

I couldn't put a word to the thing I was searching for
that divine earth-shattering crash with divinity, *anything*
I pleaded, to knock me off my ill-fated path to self-destruction
on my way to meet with my desire—*stop me in my tracks*

At first, I thought it was duty, and I wore my hands
down to the bone working for scraps—I was grateful
Next I thought it was creation, the building of worlds
and I raised the dead for my stories, told all there was to tell

Then one day, I believed with every ounce of my being
that it was a man and I was out of my mind for him
yet my body wouldn't let go in my ascension to heaven
I fell back down so hard, I almost thought I'd found it

And then on a quiet Sunday I had nothing left to give
I was still my earthly self—ashamed of my wanting
When I noticed a crack in the wall above my kitchen sink
from where a row of ants had emerged quietly one after another

Marching in a line, tiny antennas twitching, searching the ether
and all at once, a deep and profound understanding shook me
In that moment, I knew without question to be alive
is to seek and thirst and hunger. For the first time

God showed his face and I was compelled by a voice
unlike any other, coaxing me to make peace with my desire,
to remain wholly intact as I was intended—gladly imperfect—
with joy give myself up to the inevitability of my life

A Love Letter to Poetry

There is a voice inside your head
With whom you speak every night

And this voice you hear in bed
You often hear without a choice

And it sings to you as sweet as song
And will ask you nothing in return

If you're alone it stays by your side
a part of you that will never tire

And when you write, it will rejoice
For poetry is a love letter to that voice

Ask the World

When you can't find a single soul to carry your poetry to him—you must ask the whole world instead.

Mistress

His work is his mistress
He goes to her
sometimes for hours
sometimes for days

I know where he is
the minute I lose him
in mid-conversation

She's never far from his mind
His fantasy girl
Stitched from memories
of past lovers
real and imaginary

Someone

The work is sweeter when it's done to the backdrop of love. The ambient glow of knowing you are safe. Someone to bear witness to your creation. Someone to hold your hand.

Men

Men possess us like demons
like demigods
We revere them
We despise them
We chase them
We run away

We pretend we are stronger
than our desire
but we let them move
into our bodies
occupy our minds
bleed the strength from our bones
drain the charge from our spines

Men make us or they undo us
like time
like life
like love
they give us everything
They take it all

To Understand

I am only writing to you now, my sweet, because it is such a sad, sad time. And when I am sad it seems, you're the only one on my mind. The only who knows the truth depth of the deep dark sea, who has traveled as far down as me.

From the start we were bound by sadness and everything else—but you cannot live with someone who is so much like yourself. So, I am reaching out to you again, with my small, anxious hands. Because today I am not looking for kind words or platitudes—but for someone to understand.

The End of Love

Somewhere on a sidewalk
you kiss a girl hello
and the world collapses
around me as you fall into her

Somewhere on a bathroom floor
lying among the ruins of our love
I am trying to pick myself up again

Somewhere in an old abandoned house
on a distant star—they've just heard
your voice for the first time.
And if sound can go on forever
Then why can't our love?

After Thirty

For many women, turning thirty is something we are conditioned to dread. As though we are born with a clock already ticking, counting down. From our first breath, we are in a race against time.

I clearly remember my race. Looking at how far everyone had gone ahead of me, feeling panic well up in my chest. All my life, I had thought the clock ticking away inside me was a time bomb. But when the time came, I realized the clock wasn't counting down—it was counting up. And just like that, my whole life came together, and I knew it was just the beginning.

Everything good that happened after that would have happened anyway. But after thirty, I learned that when you confront your fear, it will no longer have power over you. And when you are no longer afraid, the possibilities are endless.

Night and Day

There are those who say
that love is bright
that love and hate
are day and night

Yet there is light
when darkness looms
and shadows
in every sunlit room

When grief foreshadows
the blackened moon
joy is a counter
to her doom

May we see ourselves
in every star
that sets to remind us
who we are

The Chase

I have grown soft—forgotten what it was like to go hungry. Love has spoilt me, but I don't miss a man I have to chase. Does that seem sad to you? That I don't miss you? I wish I could tell you about my life. Paint a picture of everything you're missing. Sometimes I still feel you, looking out from behind my eyes. There was a time when I would have given it all to you. But not anymore. The truth is, I loved our love more than I loved you.

Moving Time

Like love, loneliness is a nocturnal thing
when I'm missing you all night
You snatch away the sleep
You take so much time from me, my love
And what is love but a heartbeat, ticking over
What is a heartbeat but a ready and anxious clock
What are you but minute hands and hours absent
Only you can make time move for me, my love
Only you can make it stop

A Single Word

To be a poet you must hold nothing back. In poetry there is no room for ego, nowhere to hide. You must write under the pretense that no one will ever read a single word.

When We Love

Why does it hurt when we love
When love is so painfully present
Like a sheet on a line
warmed by the sun
Or when I take your hand
A simple, sweet thing
A miracle every time
You ask me why it hurts
and I breathe you in
Ever so slowly, I breathe love in
Hold it for as long as I can
and I say, ask me again
if there is tenderness in love
If there is too much of it

On Being a Muse

I need you—your warmth and despair. I want to be the word that curls around your tongue. The body that curls around your words. Sometimes it feels like a curse to be this intimate with language. To admit I am not the only one you have touched in this way.

My Love

My love calls to me
Says, when will you come back
like you promised all those years ago
When you miss the shoreline of your motherland
When you've had the world so many times over
and found it more walls than wonder
My love says I have grown old waiting for you
Don't you miss me—
not even a little?
Does this not feel like
a kind of slow death
Tell me now before I go on waiting
if I should die waiting for you

Something Back

The moment you look at me will be the end of my life. The second your arms open up for me, everything will fall to dust.

There is no such thing as happiness like this. My lips pressed into your palm. Joy tearing through me like madness. Your tongue drawing circles down my stomach. Nothing this perfect can come from God. It must be borrowed from a place so dark, it would make your skin crawl. It doesn't come without wanting something back.

The One She Loved

She lived her life hiding from herself
Trading one abuse for another
Weighing every wrong with
a feather and stone

And every man she wanted
Wanted her all to himself
and the one she loved
left her alone

Ten Things

There came a time when you were allowed only ten
worldly possessions

Down by my feet, were the things I had chosen

The first was a clock to tell the time. And to feel a heartbeat
that was separate to mine

A pencil, eraser, and book of blank pages, words written on
sand through all the ages

A spoon and bowl my fifth and sixth, a phantom meal for
me to lick

My seventh a cup to catch the rain, to quench my thirst and
dull my pain

A pillow in the place of my bed, to rest my head

My ninth, a quilt against the cold, something to hold

And when I was down to one, I couldn't choose

between a knife and a picture of you

Shame

Is it truly possible to live without shame? If not inflicted by others, then self-imposed?

Some Loves

I think of our love as a door left slightly ajar, like a magnifying glass that my hand must shield from the sun. There are some loves that are soft and gentle like the caress of summer rain and others like wild animals trapped in cages, that will devour us whole if we let them.

Those That Come

The things you want
beyond reason
how will they come?
Will it be all at once
Or one by one?

When you arrive
at your heart's desire
How will you fair?
Will it be as you imagined?
when your dream
is standing there?

There are dreams
that take a lifetime
Others—merely a day
Only those that come
too swiftly
just as quickly
slip away

All Love

It is time to do what you've always wanted. It may be the best or worst thing, but it will no doubt be the bravest. You are young enough to build your life from the ground up, old enough to know how to do it. So, close your eyes and listen to the drumming of your heart, the ringing of your soul whispering now is the time, this is now your time. Do what you must, what you must do. For those who act out of love needn't ever be afraid. I am all love and you have nothing to fear.

We Were Loved

We were loved in ways
We couldn't know
Loved with gladness
Loved with sorrow

We were taught to meet
the demands of others
In the name of love
they hurt our mothers

They kept us close
and held our hands
Gave us more love
than we could stand

And still we plead
and still we doubt
whether loved within reason
or loved without

To Yourself

Pick yourself up. Get it together. Not because others have it worse than you. Not because you owe it to anyone to put on a smile. But because you have your mother's blood flowing through your veins. And even if you think otherwise, you matter to so many people. But first of all, you need to matter to yourself.

A Reminder

People want to know you
All you have to be is present

People want to love you
All you need to be is yourself

Written

When you have written all you had to write
there is nothing left to write about but yourself

Among the Stars

A girl from nowhere special. With a fistful of dirt in her hand. And an irrepressible fire in her belly.

Who looks up at the stars and knows them by heart. Who is patiently learning the language of The Universe. And believes in something greater than herself.

That loves her unconditionally.

And will carry her always.

A girl who looks up at the stars knowing one day, she will be among them.

Show of Love

I want to buy us a house
with red roses in the yard
and a skylight above our bed
Raindrops dancing on the glass

A house made of bricks
an address that I can write to
anytime I wish
A fireplace roaring
against the long, cold night
and a blanket big enough
to wrap around us both

I think shelter is the ultimate
show of love
and I want to protect you
from everything that hurts

All the Things

You are made of the all things you have loved. You are made of the all the things you have lost. And both contribute in equal measure to your beauty and your brilliance.

Your Poetry

If I only knew you through your poetry—would ever only know you through your words—I think I would have loved you just the same.

My Version of Love

You gave me so much—I didn't know how to hold it. The moment you stopped, I was down on my knees. You said my version of love could not exist without conquest. Maybe you're right.

All my life I have fought so damn hard for every single thing I have.

If you make it too easy for me, I won't believe it's real.

This World

I love this world so very dearly
Even more so now it feels
I am losing my grip on everything
The sun came up for me even
though I never asked it to
And most days I wouldn't give
a second thought to everything
that was going right in my life.

The pure joy of waking up
with somewhere to go
something to do
and someone to love

I used to worry in the pointless way
one does—one who never had
to question her place in the world
Not knowing the fragility
of this place

Be a Poet

What is it like being a poet? You open yourself up like a big, ruinous chasm and everyone sees inside you, but no one understands who you are.

Palm

I drew on the back of my hand—all my plans. Things I would never say out loud. I stared at the words and what they meant. For myself, and everyone around. I unclenched my fist, held my palm up flat like a mirror, looked at it long and hard. I took a deep breath; my finger traced the lines from end to start. My life line. My fate line. My heart. It was all there before me like an open book, but I still didn't know what to do, even though I already knew.

Every Other Heart

Will you love me enough? Love me so much that your heart can barely hold it—that it would break every other heart you've ever held?

Good Enough

You asked me what it means
to be an artist
as I stood before you
and all the world
Took one creation
after another
lovingly conceived
painstakingly made
and with warm, trembling hands
spread them out for you
under the cruel, unforgiving light
and each new thing
was a question of whether
I was good enough

Above You

Nothing is beneath you. And if you believe this with your whole heart—believe every living soul should be treated with respect and kindness—you will realize it goes the other way.

For once you truly believe no one is beneath you—you will see no one is above.

Facade

Do you believe in fairy tales?
My once upon a time
my read between the lines

My ordinary, everyday
do you need another rhyme?
Am I just an old cliché

Did I take a wrong turn somewhere
got lost along the way
Did a year pass by each day?

You haven't asked me for some time
if I am doing fine
As long as I tack on this smile

And never show you the face behind
or tell you what's been on my mind
We can stay like this awhile

December

It is only the year that is ending. So why does it feel like the world is?

Index

Acknowledgments

I began work on *September Love* when the world was a place where we could move with freedom and ease. Like everyone else, I never considered this would change in the sudden, brutal way it has.

Touring has been an integral part of my career, and I have so many people to thank for their warmth and hospitality. I've always returned from my travels with wonderful memories in tow. Such as spotting heart-shaped traffic lights while cruising the streets of Manila with Chad and the lovely team at National Book Store. An ice cream parlor in New York with my agent Al, discussing ideas for my next novel. With Patty in Los Angeles, venturing out to Jollibee, a cult fast-food chain, beloved by Filipinos who are among my most passionate readers. A full-circle moment with my publisher Kirsty in a Sydney restaurant where, many years before, her career was set on its stunning trajectory. Exploring Chicago with Kathy, a city I'd never been to, and fell hopelessly in love with. Kuala Lumpur where Jacky and the team at Times Distribution surprised my mother with her absolute favorite—fresh durian, out of season and impossibly rare.

Last December, I found myself in a local Singaporean eatery with Zhi Wei and Carynn, the same two girls who had greeted me off the plane on my very first tour. I had no idea then, as we sat laughing and discussing our future plans, that the night would be my last real memory of normalcy.

I completed this collection after two solid months in lockdown and to the backdrop of a very different world. Tucked away in our little seaside house with my partner Michael and stepson Oliver. Some days, when the heavy fog settled over the horizon, it felt like we were the only people left in the world. The sense of isolation I'd felt during this period beautifully captured in the cover art by Tallulah Fontaine.

Yet there was never a moment where I was truly alone.

Throughout my time in lockdown, my readers were a constant source of comfort and encouragement. This book, like every other one before, is inspired by their stories of love and struggle, their everlasting hope for a kinder, softer, world. To my readers, my gratitude to you is infinite.

About the Author

Novelist and poet Lang Leav was born in a refugee camp when her family were fleeing the Khmer Rouge regime. She spent her formative years in Sydney, Australia, in the predominantly migrant town of Cabramatta. Among her many achievements, Lang is the winner of a Qantas Spirit of Youth Award, Churchill Fellowship, and Goodreads Choice Award.

Her first book, *Love & Misadventure* (2013), was a breakout success, and her subsequent poetry books have all been international best-sellers. In 2016, Lang turned her attention to fiction, and her debut novel *Sad Girls* shot to #1 on the *Straits Times* and other best-seller charts internationally.

Lang actively participates in international writers' festivals and her tours consistently draw massive crowds. With a combined social media following of two million, Lang's message of love, loss, and female empowerment continues to resonate with her multitude of readers.

Lang has been featured on CNN, SBS Australia, Intelligence Squared UK, Radio New Zealand and in various publications, including *Vogue*, *Newsweek*, the *Straits Times*, the *Guardian*, and the *New York Times*. She currently resides in New Zealand with her partner and fellow author, Michael Faudet.